NORMAL AND ABNORMAL DEVELOPMENT

NORMAL AND ABNORMAL DEVELOPMENT

The Influence of Primitive Reflexes

on Motor Development

Fourth Printing

By

MARY R. FIORENTINO, Mus. B., O.T.R.

Director of Occupational Therapy
Newington Children's Hospital
Newington, Connecticut

With a Foreword by

Myron E. Shafer, M.D.

Director, Cerebral Palsy Clinic
Newington Children's Hospital
Newington, Connecticut

CHARLES C THOMAS • PUBLISHER
Springfield • Illinois • U.S.A.

Published and Distributed Throughout the World by
CHARLES C THOMAS • PUBLISHER
BANNERSTONE HOUSE
301-327 East Lawrence Avenue, Springfield, Illinois, U.S.A.

© *1972, by* CHARLES C THOMAS • PUBLISHER

ISBN 0-398-02278-X

Library of Congress Catalog Card Number: 77-187652

First Printing, 1972
Second Printing, 1976
Third Printing, 1978
Fourth Printing, 1980

With **THOMAS BOOKS** *careful attention is given to all details of manufacturing and design. It is the Publisher's desire to present books that are satisfactory as to their physical qualities and artistic possibilities and appropriate for their particular use.* **THOMAS BOOKS** *will be true to those laws of quality that assure a good name and good will.*

Printed in the United States of America

M-3

To my Mother and Sister
Carolina and Ella Fiorentino

FOREWORD

The treatment of the cerebral palsied child has in the recent decade progressed to the point where a deeper understanding of normal reflex development and persistent primitive reflexes is a necessity for the proper treatment of these children.

This book by Miss Fiorentino now provides both physicians and therapists with a graphic representation of these reflexes. It is invaluable in the early diagnosis of the cerebral palsied child under one year of age. This book will also be a useful guide in the evaluation of newer techniques in therapy since much of this evaluation will depend upon the persistence or absence of primitive reflexes.

The information in this book has for many years been used in evaluating and treating the cerebral palsied child at Newington Children's Hospital and has been completed as a result of the demand for Miss Fiorentino to put into writing the result of her work and teaching carried on both at Newington Children's Hospital and worldwide.

MYRON E. SCHAFER

PREFACE

The developmental milestones of the normal child demonstrate the integration of the central nervous system with the lower, primitive patterns to the higher, more selective behavior necessary to the performance of everyday living.

Development of the cerebral palsied child is not normal due to the lack of integration within the central nervous system. As a result, one sees abnormal postural positioning influenced by abnormal primitive reflexes and abnormal tone. Such children, therefore, have delayed development and a lack of higher developmental function.

ACKNOWLEDGMENTS

Grateful appreciation is extended to the Newington Children's Hospital and to the Occupational Therapy Staff for their continued support and assistance; to Miss Constance M. Lundberg, O.T.R., Student Supervisor, and to Mrs. Betty Gamache, O.T.R., Assistant Director of Occupational Therapy, for their assistance in the preparation of this book; to Mr. Donald Gale, Photography Department; and to the children and parents who allowed their pictures to be used.

M.R.F.

CONTENTS

NORMAL AND ABNORMAL DEVELOPMENT

INTRODUCTION

As we know it today, cerebral palsy is the result of brain damage or maldevelopment which occurs prenatally, natally, or postnatally. This means that the lesion acts on an immature brain, interfering with its normal process of maturation and with its normal orderly development. This is evidenced by an insufficiently developed postural reflex mechanism, such as poor head control; by a lack of inhibition, demonstrated by prolonged retention of the primitive total patterns of earliest childhood, and by abnormal tone; therefore, there are impaired patterns of movement and delayed motor development.

To understand and interpret correctly the nature of the motor deficit of children with cerebral palsy, one must have a good working knowledge of normal child development. One must be able to interpret a child's functional behavior in the development of normal postural reflex mechanisms and total patterns of motor coordination. Conversely, one must study the various abnormal postural reflexes, their specific patterns of incoordination, the way in which they differ from normal primitive patterns, and the manner in which they interfere with normal motor activity.

PURPOSE

The purpose of this book is to orient physicians and therapists to the importance of knowing the developmental motor milestones as they relate to the normal child so that recognition of the lack of development as seen in the cerebral palsied child is noted at an early stage of development. The book also gives an understanding of the analysis of factors contributing to this lack of development through the persistent influence of primitive reflexes resulting in abnormal postural patterns.

PROCEDURE

The following pages present basic concepts in the maturation of normal motor development; normal motor development at certain heirarchal stages with photographs of children from the ages of six days through fourteen months, illustrating the integration and modification of primitive reflexes and postural movements to the higher, more complex functions.

The last section illustrates the effect of persistent primitive reflexes on motor development. The resultant delay is specific to the level of motor development at which the child is performing.

Chapter I

BASIC CONCEPTS IN THE MATURATION
OF NORMAL MOTOR DEVELOPMENT

MOTOR DEVELOPMENT

Normal motor development proceeds in an orderly sequence of events; from the apedal, to the quadrupedal, to the bipedal level of maturation. The central nervous system acts as a coordinating organ for the many incoming sensory stimuli, producing integrated motor responses adequate to the requirements of the environment. As the nervous system develops, more centers are established, resulting in greater possibilities of interpretation and, therefore, greater combinations of muscular actions.

Muscles are grouped in coordinated action patterns. In the performance of our everyday movements we are not conscious of the function of the individual muscles concerned with the movements, nor can we follow up or direct voluntarily every part of a movement at every stage of it, a large part of such movements being automatic, especially those of postural adjustment.

We know that from birth onward we are activated by powerful afferents. These come from the outside world through the exteroceptors such as eyes, ears, skin; internally, from the interoceptors and proprioceptors. The normal central nervous system can absorb this afferent inflow and respond according to the changing demands of the environment. The central nervous system of the cerebral palsied cannot cope as well with the demands upon it. Though the nervous system has retained its ability to respond, the afferent inflow is short-circuited into the synaptic chains of the few typical, widespread, abnormal sensorimotor patterns of movement. Thus, motor dysfunction in movement seen in the cerebral palsied child is not a result of paralysis of muscles, but to abnormal coordination, to abnormal patterning of muscle throughout the affected parts.

LEARNING OF MOVEMENTS

The learning of movements is entirely dependent upon sensory experience; sensory input which not only initiates but also guides motor output. We know from animal and human studies that sensory deprivation does alter behavior, that it does affect the central nervous system, and that we must have sensory input to have motor output. This has always been known but has not been given sufficient thought.

7

The normal child changes and modifies the sensorimotor patterns of early primitive movements and adapts them gradually to more complex functions as prehension and walking. The child can use only what he knows, e.g. what he has felt, what he has experienced, and what he can remember.

In cerebral palsy the sensorimotor experience has been abnormal from the beginning. This child can make use of his abnormal sensorimotor patterns only to the degree he may be involved.

PATTERN OF MATURATION

Human behavior follows a pattern of maturation. The normal child develops in a well-ordered sequence of events. As an infant, the nervous system receives information consisting mainly of hunger, wetness and cold, which are interpreted as harmful or unpleasant. The resultant action is crying and the mother caters to his needs. This dependency continues so that for the first eight months of his life he can do little for himself. Gradually he begins to develop basic patterns of movement and postural control by adjusting to changes of position. This continues for the first three years during which period the child learns the basic motor patterns of many skills. Later, he will use the same patterns in an increasing number of combinations, changing and adapting them to more intricate and complex functional activities.

During this process, similar modifications are seen in the primitive reflex behavior with the gradual appearance of certain automatic, postural, and adaptive reactions which make the higher activities possible.

The cerebral palsied child has immature postural reflex mechanisms plus a lack of inhibition to integrate the early patterns of movement; therefore, he has impaired patterns of movement and delayed motor development.

Chapter II

NORMAL DEVELOPMENTAL MOTOR MILESTONES

Following is a review of some of the important developmental milestones as seen in the normal child. There are two points to emphasize: (1) Development is variable even with the normal child; (2) each new activity is built upon previous patterns which are integrated and elaborated on to make possible the varied, complex, and refined movements of function.

SIX-DAY-OLD

Motor activity in the newborn, to a great extent, is a continuation of the movement of the fetus, such as the sucking reflex. Following birth, the innate aptitudes are fulfilled in the course of his anatomical and physiological development under the influence of the external environment, heredity, etc.

Rooting Reflex

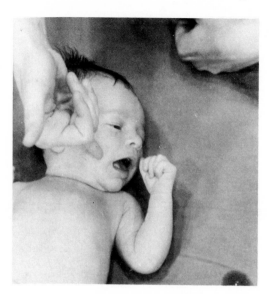

Corner of mouth lightly stroked outwards.

Result

Lower lip drops at that corner. On continuation of this contact to cheek, tongue moves towards stimulus and head turns to follow it.

Persists approximately 3–4 months, and 7 months while asleep.

Sucking Reflex

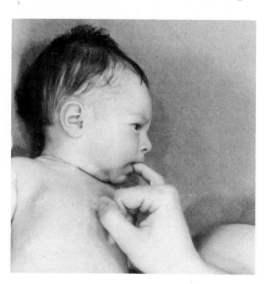

Finger placed on lips.

Result

Immediate sucking motion of lips; jaw drops and lifts rhythmically.

Persists approximately 3–4 months.

Galant (Incurvatum) Reflex

Skin stroked between twelfth rib and iliac crest.

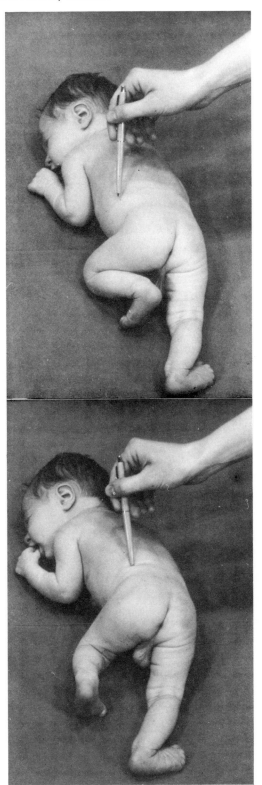

Result

Lateral flexion of the trunk toward stimulated side.

Persists approximately 2 months.

Crossed Extension Reflex

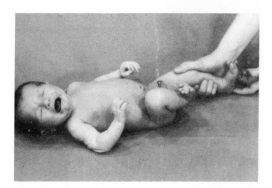

One leg held in extension; sole of foot stimulated.

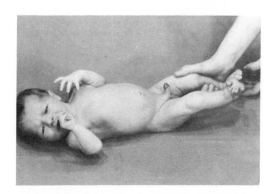

Result

Flexion, followed by extension and adduction of contralateral leg with extension and fanning of toes.

Persists approximately 1 month; weakens, then reappears in a short time.

Withdrawal Reflex

Legs extended, soles of feet stimulated.

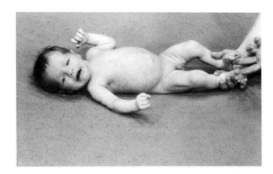

Result

Extension of toes.
Dorsiflexion of feet.

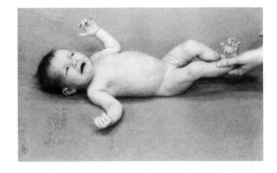

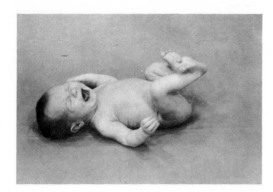

Followed by flexion of legs. Persists approximately 6–8 weeks.

Moro Reflex

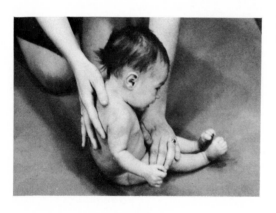

Head and shoulders raised off table. Head dropped back.

Result

Arms, fingers abducted, extended, and externally rotated. (Following first month elbows may flex.)
Followed by return to flexion for the first month.
Persists approximately 0–4 months.

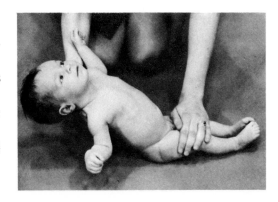

Automatic Sitting

Pressure placed on thighs and head flexed.

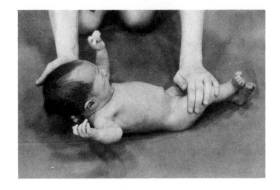

Result

Automatically rights himself.

To sitting position.

Persists   approximately   6–8 weeks.

Primary Righting Action

Infant placed on firm surface, squatting on haunches with feet flat against surface; feet pressured, ankles kneaded, or nape of neck tickled.

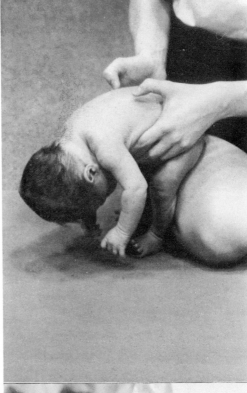

Result

Leg, trunk, and momentary head extension.

Persists approximately 6–8 weeks.

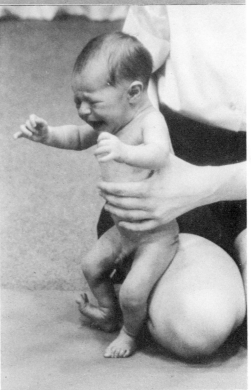

Primary Walking

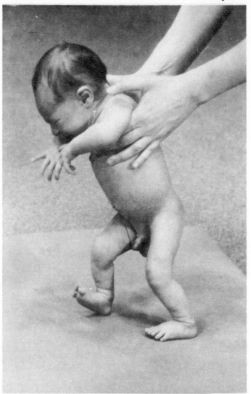

In standing position infant held under arms and inclined forward.

Results

Automatic walking steps which at this stage are rhythmical and with heel strike.

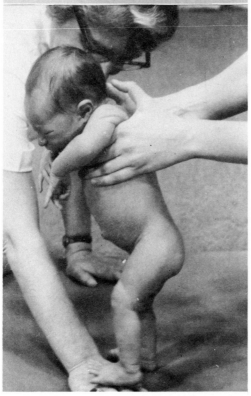

As obstacle is reached.

Automatically steps over the obstacle without faltering. (The baby also can walk up an incline plane at this time.) This primary walking persists for a variable period, up to several weeks. Then contact is made increasingly on the toes; speed, rhythm, and coordination diminish until later months.

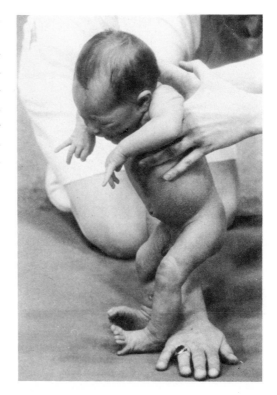

Grasp Reflex

Pressure in palm of hand approaching from ulnar side.

Result

Flexion of fingers.

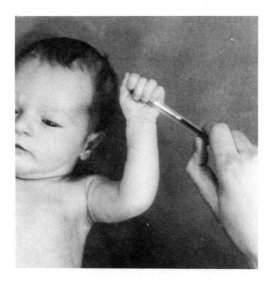

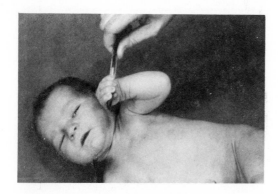

Hands pulled upward.

Result

Strong grip retained; arm does not extend.

(In a matter of weeks, arm will extend, but grasp is still strong.)

Persists approximately 3–4 months.

Finger Extension and Sequencing

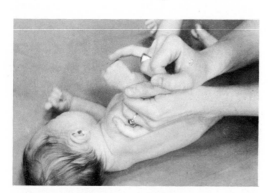

Ulnar border of palm or little finger lightly stroked.

Result

Extension of little finger followed sequentially by ring, middle, and index fingers; thumb is less mobile.

When hand closes, it does so in reverse sequential order. (This reaction is variable; usually requires summation of stimuli and does not appear immediately.)

Persists approximately 4 weeks

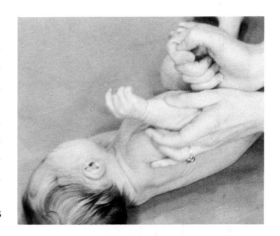

Placing Reaction

Infant held up; dorsum of hand brushed against under edge of table.

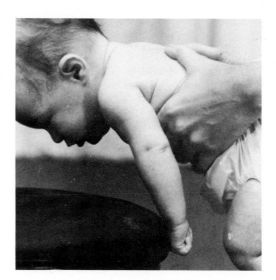

Result

Arm flexes and brings flexed hand down on table top. (At a later date, fingers are extended.)

Persists approximately 0–6 months.

Similar testing done to feet.

The results of these early tests are affected by the gestational age and physiological state of the infant and this must be considered before deciding that any reflex or reaction is or is not present. (It is suggested that other reactions, other testing methods, and more complete interpretations be investigated) [1,2,12,13,20]

At this time there is no conclusive evidence that lack of any of these reactions has a pathological significance. Nor is it known what inferences can be drawn from isolated abnormal findings; however, if certain changes are seen, especially if asymmetrical, persistent, or multiple, then it would seem logical that the child be observed carefully for any delay in development of motor movement.

SIX-WEEK-OLD

Strongly dominated by flexor tone in all positions:

Prone

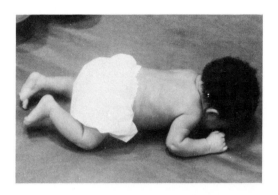

Protective, up-ended position

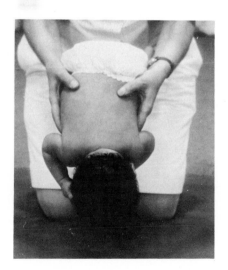

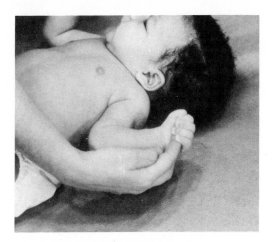

Primitive grasp and cortical thumb.

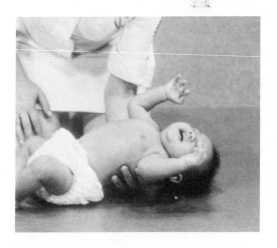

Strong Moro Reflex.

Asymmetrical Tonic Neck Reflex.

Prone head raising to 45 degrees, and neck righting to side-lying only motor development.

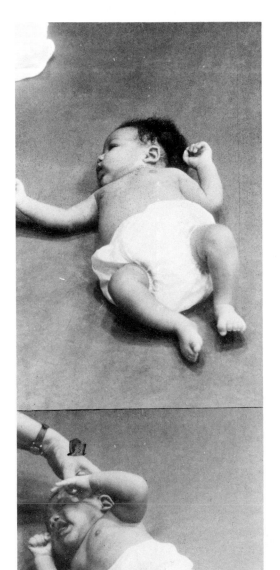

THREE-MONTH-OLD

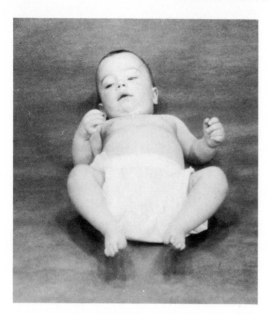

Flexor tone continues; extensor tone increasing, especially in the upper extremities and neck.

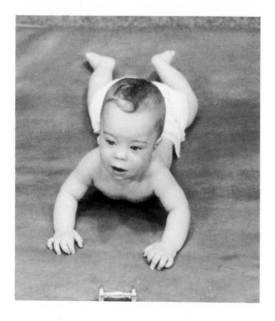

This combined with the Labyrinthine and Optical Righting on the Head enables child to extend head in prone position and assume prone-on-elbows position.

No independent sitting as there is not sufficient extensor tone in trunk and hips.

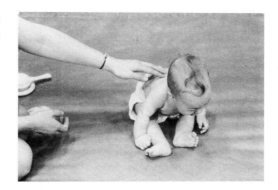

Integration of Asymmetrical Tonic Neck Reflex.

Allows voluntary positioning for hand function.

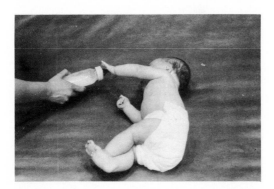

Allows voluntary neck righting.

Dominantly functions with bilateral activities at midline.

Unilateral patterns, however, are
emerging in upper extremities.

FIVE-MONTH-OLD

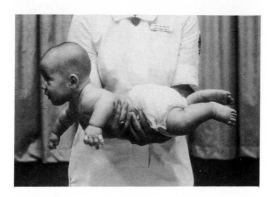

Landau Reaction is emerging increasing the extensor tone.

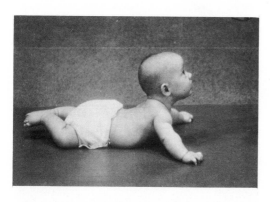

Allows baby to assume prone-on-extended-elbows position. (This is activating deep postural muscles of neck and back required for standing.)

Has rocking movements which are preparatory to crawling.

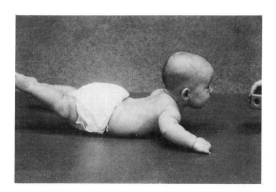

Total movement patterns of flexion and extension integrating at higher level and head is acting as independent segment; beginning to respond to Optical and Labyrinthine Righting in supine position.

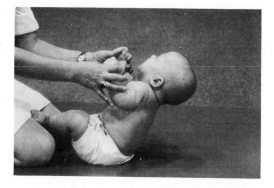

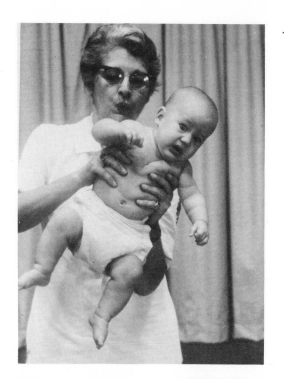

Also in lateral positions.

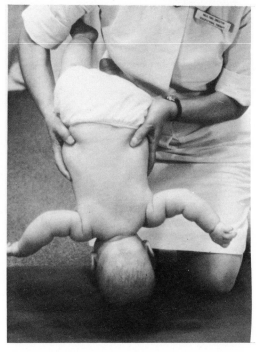

Moro Reflex persists; responds with this reaction rather than higher, automatic, Protective Extensor (Parachute) Reaction.

SIX-MONTH-OLD

Higher centers of integration now in control and this child demonstrates no primitive reactions. Moro Reflex is integrated and Protective Extensor Reaction emerges.

Now uses this Reaction for weightbearing while in sitting position. Sitting now possible as total patterns of flexion or extension have been broken up and extension of head and trunk is possible with flexion of hips.

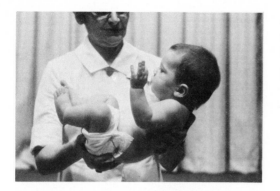

All Righting Reactions have emerged and in supine and lateral positions head rights itself past midposition.

Turning accomplished by using complete rotation from supine to prone.

Crawls forward and backward on abdomen.

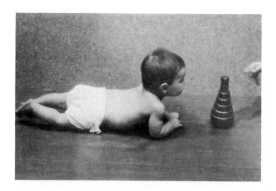

Movements now reciprocal rather than total bilateral patterns.

Sits with minimal support; manipulates toy using radial grasp.

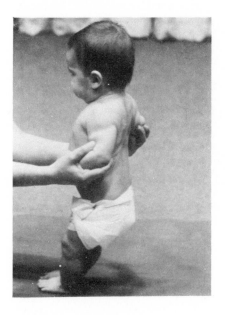

Extensor tone in hips and knees from Positive Supporting Reaction still apparent, although he can break through at will. Combined with stronger effects from the Landau Reaction, this gives firmer base of extensor tone for standing.

EIGHT-MONTH-OLD

Primitive reactions completely integrated and synthesized so that righting, protective, and equilibrium reactions available spontaneously.

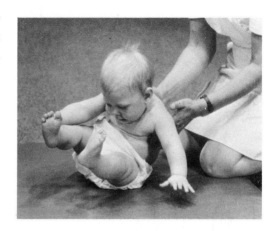

Landau Reaction still apparent for further reinforcement of extensor tone.

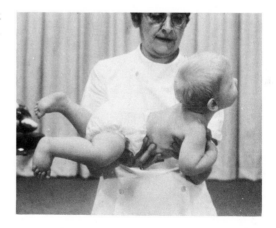

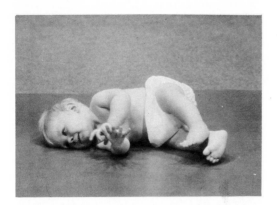

Neck righting to 4-point position.

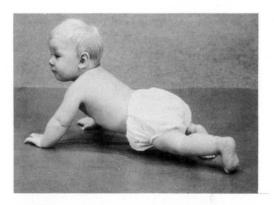

Reciprocal creeping.

Assumes sitting.

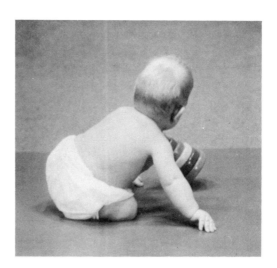

Pulls to standing and walks with support.

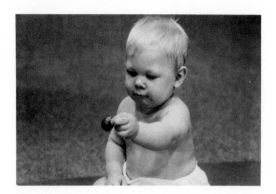

Uses pincer grasp.

FOURTEEN-MONTH-OLD

Integration of Righting and Equilibrium Reactions under cortical control which lead to varied, refined, complex movements. (This age has all basic components under cortical control for any postural adjustment needed for future motor patterns.)

Partial rotation to sitting. (Symmetrical sitting starts at approximately 4½–5 years of age).

Postural adjustments for combined movements.

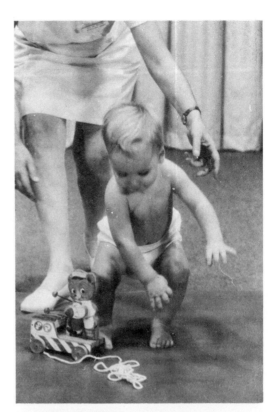

Stands independently and walks.

Has supination and opposition.

You have seen the normal, orderly, sequential development of children with intact central nervous systems. You have seen the orderly integration and synthesis of the primitive reflexes and reactions into the refined, complex movements, having all the basic components needed for any future function.

Chapter III

INFLUENCE OF PRIMITIVE REFLEXES TO MOTOR DEVELOPMENT

The persistence of primitive reflexes is shown clinically to be an influence in delaying motor development. The reflexes described in ensuing text have been found to be most prevalent in contributing to the lack in motor development.*

Crossed Extension Reflex

Extension of the flexed leg when contralateral leg is flexed.
Normal to approximately 3–4 months.

---

* Each reflex has been isolated for illustrative purposes. Most of the subjects have other reflexes, which combined, and *in toto,* place them at a stated motor level. However, for purposes of clarification, each reflex is discussed in relation to the specific developmental level illustrated and not necessarily the highest level the child has achieved.

3-year-old spastic tetraplegic

No reciprocal movement in lower extremities.
Motor development at *2-month* level.

3-year-old spastic diplegic

Can assume 4-point position, but reciprocal creeping not possible due to domination of this reflex. Motor development at *8-month* level.

6-year-old mixed spastic and athetoid

Can assume 4-point position, but cannot break through reflex for creeping.
Motor development at *8-month* level.

Tonic Labyrinthine Reflex

Flexor tone dominates in prone position; extensor tone dominates in supine position.
Normal to approximately 4 months.

3-year-old spastic tetraplegic

Cannot raise head nor pull arms from under body.
Motor development at *1-month* level.

7-year-old spastic tetraplegic

Opisthotonic position on attempts to turn.

No supine head raising; no turning.

Motor development at *4 to 5-month* level.

Asymmetrical Tonic Neck Reflex

Extensor tone on face side as head is turned; flexor tone on skull side. Normal to approximately 4–6 months.

7-year-old spastic tetraplegic

Prevents turning from supine to prone.

Motor development at *4 to 5-month* level.

4-year-old hemiplegic

Bilateral function occluded.
Motor development at *3-month*
level.

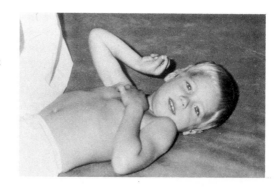

6-year-old athetoid

Can assume 4-point position, but
unable to bear weight on flexed
side as head turns. Prevents 4-
point creeping.

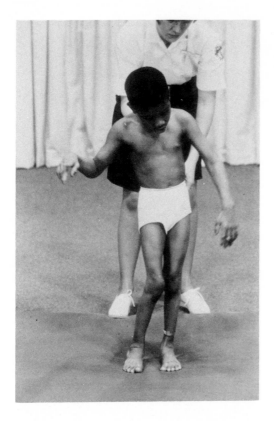

Can maintain standing and has incipient walking, but no stability on flexed side as head turns.

Motor development at *8 to 10-month* level.

Symmetrical Tonic Neck Reflex

Ventroflexion of head causes flexion in upper extremities, extensor tone in lower extremities. Dorsiflexion of head causes extension in upper extremities and flexor tone in lower extremities.

Normal to approximately 4–6 months.

6-year-old athetoid

Can assume 4-point position, but with ventroflexion of head collapses forward.

Lower extremities cannot extend.

With dorsiflexion of head extensor tone dominates upper extremities.

Flexor tone dominates lower extremities.

With either reaction, no ability to 4-point creep.

(The position of head completely controls arm and leg movements.)

Motor development at *6 to 8-month* level.

4-year-old spastic diplegic

Can assume 4-point position, but dorsiflexion of head elicits reaction in both upper and lower extremities.

Cannot 4-point creep.

(The abducted position of legs is due to release of hip adductors so that there is no stability at hips.)

Motor development at *6 to 8-month* level.

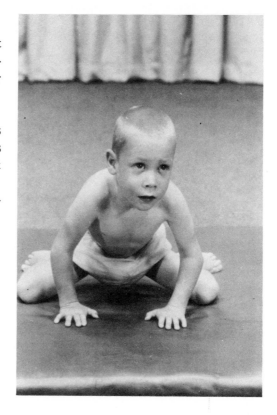

Associated Reactions

Imitation of movement in affected or other parts of body.

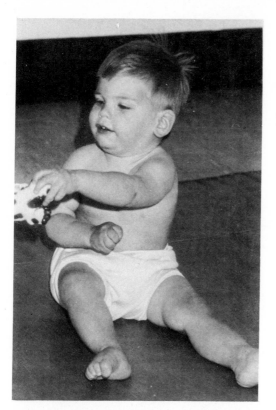

21-month-old spastic hemiplegic

Right hand similates grasping movements of noninvolved hand. Occludes bilateral function. Motor development at *6-month* level.

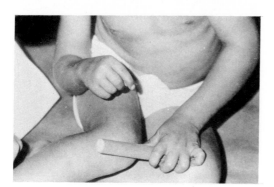

4-year-old spastic hemiplegic

Persistence of associated reactions occludes bilateral function. Motor development at *6-month* level.

Positive Supporting Reaction

Stimulation of intrinsics of feet elicits extensor tone in hips and knees, and plantarflexion of feet.
Normal starting at 3 months onto 10 months.

7-year-old spastic tetraplegic

Complete domination of this reaction results in no standing base nor reciprocal movement.
Motor development at *3 to 4-month* level.

3-year-old spastic paraplegic

Minimal influence of reflexes in supine position.

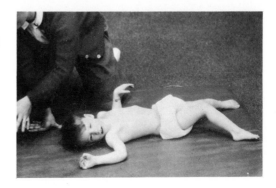

Can assume kneel-standing position.

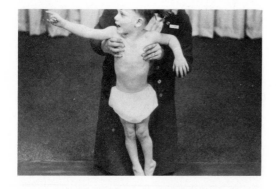

Positive Supporting Reaction as soon as placed on feet. No standing balance nor reciprocation. Motor development at *8 to 10-month* level.

3-year-old spastic paraplegic

(Heel cord lengthenings performed.) Positive Supporting Reaction persists with increase in extensor tone in hips and knees.
Reciprocation difficult.
Motor development at *10-month* level.

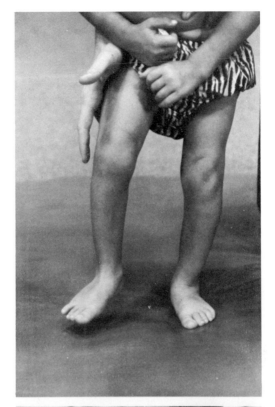

4-year-old spastic diplegic

(Adductor tenotomies performed).
Can pull to standing.
Persistence of Positive Supporting Reaction.
Reciprocation difficult.
Motor development at *10-month* level.

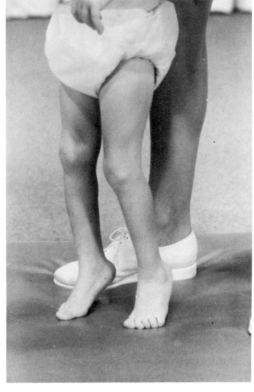

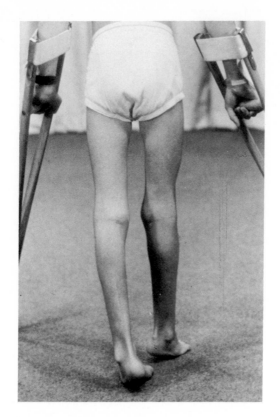

9-year-old spastic diplegic

(Medial hamstring releases, heel cord lengthenings, and Grice procedures.)

Dominated by Positive Supporting Reaction.

Walks on toes with stiff-legged gait.

No balance, reciprocation difficult.

Motor development at *10-month* level.

Moro Reflex

With sudden noise, sudden change of position, or sudden dropping back of head, arms abduct, elbows extend (or flex) , and fingers extend and abduct.

Normal to approximately 4–6 months.

4-year-old spastic diplegic

Continued domination of this reflex.
No protective reaction.

Can maintain sitting.
With sudden noise loses balance;
Moro elicited.
No protective reaction.
Motor development at *6 to 8-month* level.

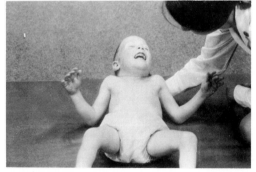

6-year-old athetoid

Can maintain standing with incipient walking.

Loss of balance elicits Moro Reflex.

No protective reaction.

Motor development at *10 to 12-month* level.

Chapter IV

EARLY DIAGNOSTIC SIGNS

The *persistence* and/or *multiplicity* of primitive reflexes and lack of higher reactions can be of diagnostic value, and can also predict the necessity for early evaluation and treatment. This six-month-old has normal development for his age level, but demonstrates a delay in certain postural reactions which could be an indication of mild hemiplegia.

Asymmetrical Tonic Neck Reflex.

Positive Supporting Reaction. (Maintains plantarflex position)

Lack of Protective Reaction on left.

Lack of Protective Reaction on the left from the sitting position.

CONCLUSION

The child with an intact central nervous system develops in an orderly, sequential manner. He develops from a being with mass movements of symmetrical synergies dominated by lower centers of primitive reactions to a child with a highly complex, integrated nervous system under cortical control with its volitional, postural, refined patterns of movement.

The child with cerebral palsy does not have an intact nervous system; therefore, he does not have an orderly developmental process. He shows a retention of the primitive reflexes and postures plus abnormal tone because of lack of sufficient integration and cortical control. Thus, he has delayed motor development.

On this basis, early evaluation and/or treatment are of the utmost importance. An attempt must be made to give these children more normal sensorimotor experience before abnormal patterns are established. It is essential to capitalize on the flexibility and pliability of the young nervous system to influence its development into more normal, sequential, postural reactions and movements. It is necessary to develop the central nervous system to its fullest potential for function. This can best be done by starting treatment in the early months of life.

BIBLIOGRAPHY

1. Andre-Thomas and Autgaerden S: *Locomotion from Pre-to Post-Natal Life.* How the newborn begins to acquire Psycho-Sensory Functions. Clinics in Developmental Medicine No. 24. The Lavenham Press Ltd., Lavenham, Suffolk, 1966.

2. Andre-Thomas, Chesni, Y., and Dargassies, S. S.: *The Neurological Examination of the Infant.* Little Club Clinics in Developmental Medicine No. 1. National Spastics Society, London, 1960.

3. Botelho, S. Y.: Proprioceptive, vestibular, and cerebellar mechanisms in the control of movement. *J. Am. Phys. Ther. Assoc., 45* (7) :667, 1965.

4. Bronisch, F. W.: The Clinically Important Reflexes. Grune, New York, 1952.

5. Buchwald, J. S.: Basic mechanisms of motor learning. *J. Am. Phys. Ther. Assoc., 45* (4) :314, 1965.

6. Eccles, J. C.: The controls of sensory communication to the brain. *Australas. Ann. Med., 31* (2) :102, 1964.

7. Eccles, J. C.: Modes of communications between nerve cells. *Science Yearbook,* 1963, p. 87.

8. Eldred, E.: Reflex plasticity in relation to posture. *Arch. Phys. Med., 46* (1–A) :10, 1965.

9. Eldred, E.: Postural integration at spinal levels. *J. Am. Phys. Ther. Assoc., 45* (4) :332, 1965.

10. Fiorentino, M. R.: *Reflex Testing Methods for Evaluating C.N.S. Development.* Springfield, Thomas 1963.

11. Held, R.: Plasticity in sensory motor systems. *Sci. Am., 213* (5) :84, 1965.

11a. Henneman, E.: Spinal reflexes and the control of movement. In *Medical Physiology,* V. M. Mountcastle, (Ed.) , 12 ed., vol. II, St. Louis, Mosby, pp. 1733–1749.

12. Illingworth, R. S.: An Introduction to Development Assessment in the First Year. Little Club Clinics in Developmental Medicine No. 3.

13. Illingworth, R. S.: *The Development of the Infant and Young Child: Normal and Abnormal (4th ed.).* Baltimore, The Williams and Wilkins Co., 1970.

14. McGraw, M. B.: *The Neuromuscular Maturation of the Human Infant.* New York and London, Hafner Pub. Co., 1963.

15. Missiuro, W.: Studies on developmental stages of children's reflex reactivity. *Child Dev., 34*:33, 1963.

16. Monie, I. W.: Development of motor behavior. *J. Am. Phys. Ther. Assoc., 43* (5) :333, 1963.

17. Moore, J. C.: *Neuroanatomy Simplified.* Dubuque, Iowa, Kendall/Hunt Pub. Co., 1969.

18. Nelson, W. E., Vaughan, V. C., and McKay, R. J.: *Textbook of Pediatrics.* Philadelphia, Pa., W. B. Saunders Co., 1969, pp. 20–57.

19. Paine, R. S. and Oppe, T. E.: *Neurological Examination of Children.* Clinics in Dev. Med. 20/21, Spastics Soc. Med. Educ. and Information Unit, William Heinemann Med. Books Ltd., 1966.

20. Peiper, A.: *Cerebral Function in Infancy and Childhood.* New York, Consultants Bureau, 1963.

21. Shy, G. M.: The plasticity of the nervous system of early childhood. *J. Am. Phys. Ther. Assoc., 45* (5) :437, 1965.

22. Twitchell, T. E.: Normal motor development. *J. Am. Phys. Ther. Assoc., 45* (5):419, 1965.

23. Twitchell, T. E.: Variations and abnormalities of motor development. *J. Am. Phys. Ther. Assoc., 45* (5) :424, 1965.

24. Zappella, M., Foley, J., and Cookson, M.: The placing and supporting reactions in children with mental retardation. *J. Ment. Defic. Res., 8* (1) :1, 1964.

INDEX